PLAY & LEARN
WITH PAPER SHAPES
& BORDERS

Written and Compiled by the Totline Staff
Illustrated by Gary Mohrmann

TOTLINE® BOOKS

Warren Publishing House
Everett, Washington

We wish to thank the following teachers, parents, and childcare workers who contributed ideas to this book: Barbara Backer, Charleston, SC; Ellen Bedford, Bridgeport, CT; Karen Blaser, Alliance, OH; Janice Bodenstedt, Jackson, MI; Cindy Brengman, Everett, WA; Cindy Dingwall, Palatine, IL; Barbara Dunn, Hollidaysburg, PA; Laura Egge, Lake Oswego, OR; Rita Galloway, Harlingen, TX; Ellen Javernick, Loveland, CO; Laura H. Nass, Twin Falls, ID; Susan M. Paprocki, Northbrook, IL; Beverly Qualheim, Marquette, MI; Debbie Rowley, Redmond, WA; Shannon Shorey, Orlando, FL; Betty Silkunas, Lansdale, PA; Diane Thom, Maple Valley, WA; Kathy Thompson, Sioux Falls, SD; Deborah Zumbar, Alliance, OH.

EDITORIAL STAFF:
    Editorial Manager: Kathleen Cubley
    Editors: Kate Ffolliott, Susan Hodges
    Contributing Editors: Gayle Bittinger,
      Elizabeth McKinnon, Jean Warren
    Copy Editor: Mae Rhodes
    Proofreader: Kris Fulsaas

PRODUCTION STAFF:
    Art Managers: Uma Kukathas, Jill Lustig
    Book Design/Layout: Carol Debolt, Lynne Faulk
    Cover Design/Layout: Brenda Mann Harrison
    Production Manager: Jo Anna Brock

ISBN 1-57029-027-X

Library of Congress Catalog Card Number 95-60004
Printed in the United States of America
Published by: Warren Publishing House
        P.O. Box 2250
        Everett, WA 98203

20 19 18 17 16 15 14 13 12 11 10 9 8 7 6 5 4 3 2 1

INTRODUCTION

Playing and learning go hand in hand for children. That's why your children will love doing the activities in this book.

Die-cut paper shapes (sometimes called calendar shapes or cutouts) and bulletin board borders are favorites at most parent-teacher supply stores. These teaching aids are available in a variety of colors, shapes, and sizes. Printed and plain, large and small—paper shapes are even available as self-stick notepads. Borders also vary: corrugated and smooth, printed and plain, cut into scallops or shapes—there are borders to fit almost any occasion. These inexpensive materials are great for easy, convenient room decorating. With a little creativity and the help of this book, they can become much more.

In this book, you will find over 100 ideas for using these innovative products to extend every area of your curriculum. From art and language to math and music, paper shapes and borders can be the basis for enjoyable learning opportunities.

Once you start creating with paper shapes and borders, you'll be amazed at the new ideas that follow. There are unlimited uses for these familiar supplies. We believe that the ideas in this book will prove to be exciting and successful, both for you and your children.

CONTENTS

PAPER SHAPES

BORDERS

ART

Finger Puppets

Let each of your children select an animal or character paper shape. Fold each shape up from the bottom and cut two half circles on the crease. Unfold the shape, showing two circles in the "body" of the shape. Show the children how to place their index and second fingers through the holes and walk the Finger Puppets around. Encourage the children to act out scenes together with their different finger puppet characters.

HINT: To make the puppets more durable, attach them to index cards and trim along the outline of each shape before cutting the finger holes.

Stick Puppet Stage

Place one long side of a shoebox on a flat surface with the open side facing you. Cut a rectangular slit in the long side of the box. Let your children decorate the box. Make quick character puppets by attaching paper shapes to the ends of craft sticks. Insert these puppets up through the slit in the box so that they show through the opening. Encourage the children to make up plays to perform on this puppet stage.

EXTENSION: Make curtains for the stage using colored tissue paper.

Simple Butterfly Puppet

Collect a butterfly paper shape for each of your children. Encourage the children to decorate their butterfly shape in any way they wish. You may want to set out glitter, colored paper, and glue for this purpose. After the children have decorated the shapes, show them how to gently bend the wings upward. Then help them attach the body of their butterfly to the end of a craft stick. Have the children "fly" around the room with their butterfly puppets as you play quiet music.

Making Necklaces

Set out a variety of paper shapes, dried tube-shaped pasta (such as rigatoni), and a 2-foot length of yarn for each of your children. Punch one hole in the center of each shape. Tie a piece of pasta to one end of each length of yarn to prevent the shapes and pasta from sliding off. Help the children string the shapes and pasta in various sequences to create designs. When they have strung nearly the length of the yarn, help the children tie the ends of the yarn together to form a necklace.

EXTENSION: Create theme or seasonal necklaces, for example, a Hawaiian lei with flower shapes, a farm necklace with barnyard shapes, or a harvest necklace with pumpkin shapes.

Three-Dimensional Designs

Gather paper shapes representing things that can jump or fly, such as rabbits, frogs, butterflies, or birds. Set out the shapes and precut 1-by-5-inch paper strips. Have each child select a shape and a paper strip. Help the children accordion-fold their paper strip. Then have them attach one end of the folded strip to a shape (if there are designs on your shapes, be sure the printed side faces out). Attach the other end of the folded strip to a bulletin board. The shapes will appear to jump out at you.

Sewing Shapes

For each of your children, cover a large paper shape with clear self-stick paper. Punch holes along the outside of each shape. Tie a length of yarn through one hole on each shape and wrap tape around the other end of the yarn to make a "needle." Show the children how to sew their shapes by pushing the needle up through one hole and down through the next.

Constellations

Explain to your children that a constellation is a group of stars in the sky that has a special name and shape. The Big Dipper is a constellation that looks like a ladle. Other constellations look like a swan, a bear, or a fish. Set out a large piece of butcher paper, star shapes, and tape or glue. Let the children work together to use the stars to create their own constellations on the paper. Encourage them to name their constellations.

Create a Creature

Gather a variety of shapes that represent animals or other creatures. Snip off the tails, heads, legs, and so on, from each shape. Set out the combination of cut shapes and tape or glue. Give each of your children a piece of plain paper. Have them select whatever combination of animal parts they like and assemble them into make-believe creatures. Encourage the children to name their creations.

Hearty Creatures

Collect various sizes of heart shapes in different colors. Set out glue and the heart shapes. Let your children glue the hearts together any way they wish to create Hearty Creatures. Have them add details with crayons. For instance, the hearts could be wings on a butterfly or ears for a dog, or the face of an imaginary creature.

Texture Bears

For each of your children, place three bear shapes on a piece of construction paper. Have the children cover the bears with glue. Set out a variety of materials of different textures, such as rinsed, dried coffee grounds; rice; cotton balls; or sand. Let each child choose three materials to sprinkle on the shapes, one on each bear. When the glue dries, shake off the excess.

Cooperative Quilt

Lay out a large piece of butcher paper on a table or on the floor. Give each of your children a plain piece of paper. Have your children glue their favorite shapes to their piece of paper in any design they wish. When they are finished decorating, attach each child's paper to the butcher paper and hang the paper on a wall or bulletin board. Explain to the children that what makes their work a patchwork quilt is that each piece of paper, or patch, makes up part of the design when put together. Display the quilt on the wall and ask the children if they can identify their portion of the design.

Bookmark Gifts

Cut construction paper into 3-by-7-inch strips. Set out a variety of paper shapes. Help your children glue or tape the shapes to the strips in their own design. Help them write their name on the back. Then cover the bookmarks with clear self-stick paper. For a finishing touch, punch a hole in the top of each bookmark and tie on a loop of colorful yarn.

EXTENSION: Follow the same instructions on a full piece of construction paper to make a placemat.

Make a Flag

Show your children pictures of flags from around the world. Explain that national flags have designs made up of colors and shapes that identify countries. Then give each child a piece of construction paper and set out a variety of paper shapes. Have the children design their own flags by attaching the shapes to the paper in any arrangement they desire. When the children have finished their flag designs, help them add flag "poles" by attaching long, thin pieces of cardboard or cardboard tubes to one edge of their designs. Display the original flags on the wall.

Dress-Up Shapes

Let your children use colorful construction paper scraps to make clothing for their favorite character shapes. For instance, they could make a hat for a bear or a bathing suit for a whale. Help the children attach the clothes to their favorite shapes.

VARIATION: Design clothing appropriate for various types of weather. During opening activities, dress a character shape according to the day's weather.

Framing Fun

Have your children create artwork on small pieces of paper before beginning this activity. Collect a variety of large paper shapes and have each child choose one. Cut a square from the center of each paper shape (fold the shape down the middle to make it easier to cut). Then help the children place their paper shape over their small piece of artwork so the art shows through the square.

VARIATION: Frame photographs of your children with paper shapes.

Rubbing Surprise

Collect a sheet of paper and a self-stick removable paper shape for each of your children. Fold each paper in half and place a shape in the middle of one half, as if it were being placed inside a greeting card. Staple the piece of paper shut along all three open edges. Set these papers and assorted crayons out for your children. Help the children rub over the paper with the side of a peeled crayon and watch the surprise shape appear.

LANGUAGE

Roll-a-Story Cube

Fill the sides of a photograph cube with various paper shapes. Let your children take turns rolling the cube and naming the shape that lands on top. Incorporate the animal or object shape into a group story.

VARIATION: Use a sturdy cube-shaped box instead of a picture cube.

Silly Story

At group time, put as many paper shapes as you have children into a paper bag. Pass the bag around the circle and have each of your children select one shape. Let each child make up a sentence about the shape he or she has selected. Write the sentences on a chalkboard or on a piece of butcher paper. When all the sentences have been heard, read the story back to the children, having them hold up their shape when it is mentioned. (Note that the story may not make sense.)

Magic Movable Characters

Choose a story that features animal characters and select paper shapes to represent the animals in the story. Crease each animal shape at the bottom so that it can stand. Attach a large paper clip to the bottom of each animal shape. Turn a thin cardboard box upside down so that the open end faces down. Place one of the characters on top of the box. Put your arm through the opening at the bottom of the box and hold a strong magnet under the paper clip on the character. Move the character by moving the magnet as you tell the story. Show your children how to use these Magic Movable Characters.

Original Story

Set out construction paper and a variety of scenic pictures cut from magazines. Have each of your chilren glue a magazine scene to a piece of construction paper. When the children have finished, stack the construction paper sheets and staple them along the left edge to form the pages of a book. Let your children choose a self-stick removable paper shape for a character. Encourage your children to help you make up a story as you move the character from one scene to the next.

VARIATION: Older children may enjoy drawing their own scenes.

A 🦋 named Beatrice once lived in the 🌳🌳🌳. She was a lonely 🦋 and would fly from 🌼 to 🌼 looking for other 🦋🦋. Sometimes Beatrice would fly so high in the sky she could almost touch a ☁. But she still could not find another 🦋.

One day it began to 🌧. When the 🌧 stopped the ☀ came out and soon Beatrice could see a colorful 🌂 far away. She flew and flew until she came close to the 🌂, where Beatrice saw that it was not a 🌂 at all, but many beautiful 🦋🦋 flying about. Beatrice joined in with her new 🦋 friends and was never lonely again.

Shape a Book

Collect a variety of paper shapes and write a simple story that incorporates those shapes. Print the story on a large piece of butcher paper, replacing words with appropriate paper shapes wherever possible. Read the story aloud to your children, pointing out each word as you read it. When you come to a paper shape, encourage the children to help you "read" those words.

Sitting-in-a-Tree Book

Set out an assortment of paper shapes, making sure that there are no duplicates. Draw a simple tree on a plain piece of paper and make a photocopy for each of your children. Have each child choose a paper shape and attach it to his or her paper so that the shape appears to be sitting in the tree. Then gather all the pages together and staple them along the left edge to form a book. Use the book for the following repetitive language activity.

Show your children the first page of the book. If the page contains a pink pig, then you would say, "Pink pig, pink pig, what could it be?" Turn to the next page. If the second page features a teddy bear, then the response would be, "I see a teddy bear sitting in our tree. Teddy bear, teddy bear, what do you see?" Turn to the following page and continue until all the shapes have been included in the rhyme. After a few pages, your children will be able to recite the rhyme with you. When you reach the end of your book, finish with the words, "There's no one else sitting in our tree."

Rhyming Game

Place approximately ten paper shapes in a bag. Have your children sit in a circle. Let each child in turn choose a shape from the bag and say the name of the shape. Encourage the group to think of a word that rhymes with that shape name. For instance, for a tree shape, possible answers could include *knee* or *free*.

Alphabet Cover-Up

On a piece of posterboard, print a few alphabet letters that you are working on. Choose a paper shape to represent each of those letters. For example, you might choose an apple shape for *A*, a bear shape for *B*, a cake shape for *C*, and so on. Print the corresponding letter on each shape. You may wish to cover the shapes with clear self-stick paper for durability. Encourage your children to place each of the shapes on the matching letter on the posterboard. Add more letters and shapes as your children learn to recognize more alphabet letters.

LEARNING GAMES

Big and Small

Many paper shapes come in both a large size and a small size. Collect several sets of shapes in both sizes. Mix up the shapes and let your children match each large shape with its corresponding small shape.

Magnet Match-Up

Collect several paper shapes in assorted shapes and colors. Attach a magnetic strip to the back of each shape and cover the shape with clear self-stick paper. Set out the shapes near a magnetic surface such as a refrigerator or a nonaluminum baking pan. Put a shape on the magnetic surface. Ask one of your children to put a shape of the same color beneath it. Continue with the remaining colors. On another day, let your children try matching the pieces according to shape.

VARIATION: Once the children have mastered this game, try a more challenging version. Name a color and have the children put all the shapes of that color on the magnetic surface.

Pairing Up

Collect enough pairs of different paper shapes so that each of your children can have one shape. Then shuffle the paper shapes. Have your children spread out around the room and ask them to close their eyes. Give each child a paper shape. After handing out all the shapes, ask the children to open their eyes and look for a child holding a paper shape that matches theirs. Let the pairs of children whose shapes match be partners for the next activity.

Paper Shape Lotto

Make a gameboard by dividing a 9-inch square of posterboard into nine equal sections. Gather nine different paper shapes. Glue a different paper shape to each of the sections on the gameboard. Glue nine matching paper shapes to another 9-inch posterboard square that has been divided into nine sections. Cut the sections apart to make game cards. To play, have your children place the game cards on top of the matching shapes on the gameboard.

Pattern Fun

Arrange four self-stick removable shapes in a row on a chalkboard or other surface. Set out an assortment of self-stick removable shapes, including some that match those on the chalkboard. Let your children take turns picking from these shapes to repeat the pattern below yours. When everyone has had a chance, repeat the game with a new pattern.

VARIATION: Attach loops of tape turned sticky-side out to shapes instead of using self-stick removable shapes.

Fill in the Blanks

Using two different self-stick removable paper shapes, create several lines of an "A-B-A-B-A" pattern on a piece of construction paper. Each time you repeat the pattern, leave out the first, middle, or last shape and draw in a blank line. Give the paper to one of your children, along with several of the paper shapes in the pattern. Let the child complete the patterns by sticking the appropriate shapes in the blanks.

Puzzle Swap

Glue a variety of shapes to thin cardboard. Cut around each shape with scissors. Then cut each shape into interlocking pieces. Make a puzzle for each of your children. After the children have pieced their puzzles together, have them swap puzzles with a partner and try again.

HINT: When making puzzles for young children, a good guideline is to cut as many pieces as years of age. For example, you might make three-piece puzzles for 3-year-olds or four-piece ones for 4-year-olds.

Number Puzzles

Cut several different paper shapes into halves. Mark one half of each shape with a numeral and the other half with the corresponding number of dots. Have your children match the halves to reinforce number concepts.

VARIATION: Make puzzles with upper- and lower-case letters instead of numerals and dots.

Counting Mobiles

Use a coat hanger and thread to make a simple mobile with dangling numerals and shapes. Choose a shape for each number you want to reinforce. Print the numerals in block lettering on construction paper, and then cut them out. Punch one hole in the top and the needed number of holes in the bottom of each numeral. Hang the numerals from a coat hanger using thread. Then hang the corresponding number of identical shapes from each numeral. For example, hang one leaf shape from the numeral 1. Hang two bunny shapes from the numeral 2, and so on. As your class learns to count to higher numbers, make more mobiles and hang them around the room. Ask your children such questions as, How many leaves are there? How many bunnies are there? Are there more leaves than bunnies?

Flower Subtraction

Attach pieces of felt to five flower shapes. Place the flowers in a row on a flannelboard. As your children sing the following song, have one of them remove a flower as indicated until none remain.

Sung to: "The Paw-Paw Patch"

Five little flowers growing in my garden.
Five little flowers growing in my garden.
Five little flowers growing in my garden.
Jannel picked one, and then there were four.

Substitute the name of one of your children for *Jannel* and the appropriate numbers for *five* and *four* in each verse.

Barbara Backer

Animals in the Barns

Gather three large paper barn shapes and attach them in a row to a piece of butcher paper. Collect three different self-stick removable farm animal shapes such as a pig, a lamb, and a cow. Give the shapes to your children. Talk about the order of the barns. Explain that the barn farthest to the left is "first," the barn in the middle is "second," and the barn to the right is "third." Then let the children place the animals on the barns as you give directions such as, Put the pig in the second barn, Put the lamb in the third barn, and so on.

Bunny Hop

Collect a bunny shape for each of your children. Write a familiar numeral on each shape. Have the children sit in a circle. Place a shape face down in front of each child. To start the game, call out the name of one child. Have that child pick up his or her bunny shape, identify the number on it, and place it back on the floor. Then, while you sit down in that child's place, have him or her hop that number of times from child to child to determine who gets the next turn. Continue until each child has had a turn to do the Bunny Hop.

Numeral Match

For each of your children, divide a piece of plain paper into five sections. Number the sections 1 through 5, and put the corresponding number of dots by each number. Set out glue and a selection of paper shapes. Help your children attach matching numbers of shapes to their sections. For example, have them glue one heart in the 1 section, two bears in the 2 section, and so on.

Counting Worms

Collect five large apple shapes. Cut one hole in the first shape, two holes in the second, and so on. Mark each shape with the numeral that represents the number of holes in it. Let your children take turns choosing an apple shape, sticking their fingers through the holes, and naming the number of "worms" they see in each apple.

Five Little Whales

Attach five paper whale shapes to a wall. Write the numerals 1 through 5 on the shapes, in order. As you and your children recite the following rhyme, have one child remove one whale for each verse until no whales remain.

Five little whales were shaking their tails,

All on a summer's day.

A shark came by and gave them the eye,

And one whale swam away.

Repeat, each time substituting the remaining number of whales for *five*.

Barbara Backer

Counting Leaves

Cut five large squares out of heavy paper. On each square draw a bare tree. Write a numeral from 1 to 5 under each tree. Collect 15 small paper leaf shapes. Set out the tree cards and the leaf shapes. Have one of your children identify the numerals beneath the trees and place the corresponding number of leaves on them.

Shape Folder

On the inside of a file folder, trace around the outlines of eight different paper shapes. Then place the shapes randomly in the open folder on a table. Let your children match the shapes by placing the paper shapes inside the matching outlines. Store the paper shapes in an envelope taped to the back of the folder for convenience.

Four Little Stars

Attach four star shapes to a bulletin board. As you recite the following poem, remove the stars one at a time.

Four little stars winking at me,
One shot off, then there were three.

Three little stars with nothing to do,
One shot off, then there were two.

Two little stars afraid of the sun,
One shot off, then there was one.

One little star not having any fun,
It shot off, then there were none.

VARIATION: Use self-stick removable star shapes on any surface, if available.

Jean Warren

Five Little Sheep

Attach five sheep shapes to a bulletin board. Let your children take turns removing the shapes as you read the poem that follows.

Little Bo Peep had five little sheep
That played by the cottage door.
One ran away while out at play,
Then Little Bo Peep had four.

Little Bo Peep had four little sheep
That played by the old oak tree.
One ran away while out at play,
Then Little Bo Peep had three.

Little Bo Peep had three little sheep
That played with Little Boy Blue.
One ran away while out at play,
Then Little Bo Peep had two.

Little Bo Peep had two little sheep
That played all day in the sun.
One ran away while out at play,
Then Little Bo Peep had one.

Little Bo Peep had one little sheep
That played all day and had fun.
It ran away while out at play—
Now Little Bo Peep has none.

Jean Warren

Simple Counting Books

Make a blank book for each of your children by stapling ten pieces of plain paper together with a construction paper cover. Write "My Counting Book" and the child's name on the front. Use a crayon or felt tip marker to number the pages of each book from 1 to 10. Set out an assortment of paper shapes and glue. Then have the children identify the numerals on their book pages and glue on corresponding numbers of paper shapes.

VARIATION: For younger children, number the book pages with numerals and sets of dots.

I'm Thinking of Something

Have your children sit with you in a group. Place a variety of paper shapes in a paper bag. Draw a shape from the bag and keep it a secret. Give the children hints about what the shape is. For instance, for an apple shape say, "I'm thinking of something round and red." Let your children take turns guessing what the object is. If no one guesses correctly, give another clue. Let the first child to correctly name the object keep that shape.

Memory Game

Arrange three or four different self-stick removable shapes on a wall or chalkboard. Have your children close their eyes while you remove one of the shapes. Sing the following song and then have the children guess which shape is missing.

Sung to: "Frère Jacques"

There is one, there is one
Shape gone, shape gone.
Can you tell me which one,
Can you tell me which one
Is gone, is gone?

Gayle Bittinger

Star Colors

Color each tip of a large paper star a different color. Attach the star to a piece of cardboard, cover it with clear self-stick paper, and trim the edges. Then color the ends of five spring-type clothespins to match the colors on the star points. To play the game, let your children take turns clipping the clothespins to the matching star points.

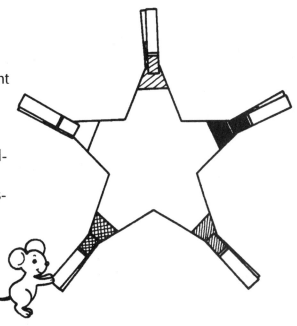

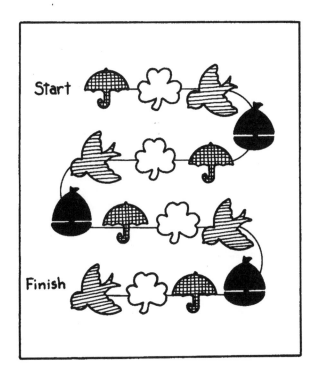

Shape Board Game

Make a gameboard for each group of two or three children. In the upper left-hand corner of a large piece of construction paper, print *Start*. Then tape a path of paper shapes in random order winding around and down the paper. End in the lower left-hand corner by printing *Finish*. Make three or four game cards for each shape by gluing shapes to index cards. Put the cards in a pile face down and give each of your children a different kind of game marker to place at Start. As each child turns up a card, have that child move his or her marker to the next shape indicated by the card. Have the children continue playing until everyone has reached Finish.

Search for Your Star

Write the names of your children on paper star shapes. Arrange the stars around the room. As you sing "Twinkle, Twinkle, Little Star," have your children search for their star. When each child has found his or her star, sing the song together.

Gone Fishing

Gather pairs of fish shapes of different colors. Glue matching pairs together with a paper clip inside. Tie 2 feet of string to a paper towel tube, wooden spoon, or ruler to make a fishing pole. Attach a magnet to the end of the string for a "hook." Place the fish shapes in a large box. Give one of your children the fishing pole. Let the child try to "catch" a fish by touching the magnet to the paper-clipped fish. Ask the child to catch a fish of a particular color or a certain number of fish. Continue until each child has caught a fish.

Shape Outlines

Set out pieces of construction paper, an assortment of paper shapes, and loops of tape rolled sticky-side out. Have each of your children select several shapes and a sheet of construction paper. Let your children tape their shapes to their papers. Show your children how to use the wide part of a peeled crayon to rub over their shapes to make rubbings. Then have the children remove their shapes and swap their shapes and paper with a partner. Let the children try to match their partner's shapes to the outlines made by the rubbings.

Little Puzzles

For a simple matching game, cut a variety of paper shapes in half horizontally or vertically. Mix up the shape halves and encourage your children to reassemble them.

SCIENCE

Measuring Fun

Gather together several shapes of the same kind. Ask one of your children to guess how long something in the room is in terms of that shape. For instance, ask the child how many bell shapes he or she thinks it would take to reach across the table. Then encourage the children to line up the shapes along the edge of the table and see how many shapes it actually takes to span the length.

Mirror Shapes

Cut a variety of paper shapes in half. Give each of your children a hand mirror and a paper shape half. Have the children place their paper shape half on a table. Let them experiment with holding their hand mirrors next to their half-shapes to make the halves appear to be whole.

Birthday Chart

Make a chart that includes a column under every month of the year. Have your children gather around the chart. As you call out each month, have all the children with a birthday in that month raise their hand. Use a birthday cake shape to indicate each child with a birthday in each month. When the cake chart is complete, ask your children questions such as, Which month has the most birthdays? Which month has the fewest? How many birthdays are in May?

Mystery Shape Book

Cut 2 inches off the tops of several paper lunch bags that you have kept folded flat. Stack the bags on top of one another with all the flap folds to the right. Then staple the bags together on the left-hand side to make a book. Tape a different paper shape under each flap in each bag so that only part of the shape is visible when the flap is closed. As your children go through the book, have them look at the part of each shape that is showing and try to predict what shape is hidden beneath the flap before lifting it up.

MUSIC & MOVEMENT

Musical Shapes

Collect an assortment of farm animal shapes, making sure you have one shape for each of your children (repeats of animals are fine). Place the shapes in a circle on the floor. Invite the children to stand in a circle around the shapes. Play music and have the children walk around the circle. When you stop the music, have the children look down and notice what animal shape they are standing in front of. Then ask the children who are standing near a particular animal to make the noise that animal would make. For instance, have all of the cows moo, the pigs oink, then the sheep baa, and so on. Continue until everyone has had a chance to make every animal noise.

Did You Ever See?

Sung to: "Did You Ever See a Lassie?"

Did you ever see a shape,

> *(Adult sings while pointing to a shape.)*

A shape, a shape?

Did you ever see a shape

Like this one before?

The shape is a star,

> *(Everyone sings.)*

The shape is a star.

Oh yes, we've seen a shape

Like that one before.

Substitute the name of a different paper shape for *star* in each verse.

Laura Egge

Shapely Moves

From an assortment of paper shapes, make shape necklaces for your children by punching a hole in a shape and tying yarn through the hole. Distribute the necklaces among your children. Now invite the children to stand in a circle wearing their necklaces. Sing the following song with them.

Sung to: "If You're Happy and You Know It"

If you've got a bunny shape, jump so high.

> *(Children wearing bunny necklaces jump in place.)*

If you've got a bunny shape, jump so high.

If you've got a bunny shape,

If you've got a bunny shape,

If you've got a bunny shape, jump so high.

Continue with verses for each of the remaining necklaces. For example, If you've got a star shape, reach for the sky; If you've got a fish shape, swim so deep.

Susan Hodges

Do You Know?

Sung to: "The Mulberry Bush"

Children, children, do you know,

> *(Adult sings while holding up a shape.)*

Do you know, do you know,

Children, children, do you know

The shape I'm holding up?

> *(Children name shape.)*

Hold up a different shape for each verse.

Laura Egge

⬛ TIPS

Personalized Parent Calendar

Have each of your children make a collage each month using seasonal shapes. Help them write their name on their collage. Then mount your parent calendar or any messages that you have for parents on the back of the children's collages. The parents will then be more likely to pay close attention to the materials you send home for them.

Flannelboard Tip

To use paper shapes on flannelboards, simply glue a small piece of sandpaper to the back of each shape. The sandpaper will adhere the shape to the felt. Keep these shapes in a small box next to the flannelboard so your children can use them during free play.

Felt Patterns

To make felt patterns quickly without time-consuming tracing, use paper shapes as patterns. Simply place the paper shape you want to copy on the felt and cut around it. You will have numerous pattern pieces at your fingertips.

Storage Identification

If you store teaching materials in covered boxes, use paper shapes to label holiday or seasonal items. Glue an appropriate shape on all sides of a box for easy identification.

Party Tip

Make a quick party decoration by placing a pair of shapes around the top of a drinking straw. Secure the shapes with tape and hand the straws to your children.

Decorating Cakes

Make designs on cakes with this easy tip. Place a pattern of shapes on a sheet cake. Sprinkle powdered sugar over the entire surface of the cake. (If the cake is white, use cocoa instead of powdered sugar.) Carefully remove the shapes and enjoy the pattern you have made.

Birthday Fun

Use birthday cake shapes to help celebrate a child's birthday. Attach the cake shape on or near the birthday child's cubby for a birthday greeting.

VARIATION: Use self-stick removable cake shapes. To make the cake shape appear to stand up, crease it just above the adhesive strip.

Attendance Chart

To create a simple attendance chart, first set aside a section of a magnetboard for the chart. Write each of your children's names on a paper shape and cover the shapes with clear self-stick paper. Attach a piece of magnetic strip to each shape, and place a basket near the magnetboard. As the children arrive each day, have them go to the basket and look for their name. Then have them attach their name shape to the board. When the day begins, you will be able to tell at a glance who is absent by looking at the names that remain in the basket. At the end of the day, have your children return their names to the basket before going home.

Handy Reminders

Use hand shapes to encourage healthy habits. On a series of paper hand shapes, draw pictures that show times when children should wash their hands. For example, you might draw pictures reminding children to wash their hands before snack, after art, and after using the restroom. Cover the hand shapes with clear self-stick paper and display them near the sink as a reminder of good hygiene.

VARIATION: Draw pictures to remind children of the steps in the hand washing process.

Speedy Nametags

Use paper shapes to make quick nametags for your children or for guests who visit your classroom. Print the child's or visitor's name on a shape and then attach the shape to that person's clothing.

Turn-Taking Tip

For each of your children, glue a paper shape to the underside of a carpet square. Make sure that all of the shapes but one are the same. Distribute the squares, shape-side down, in a circle. Play or sing music and have the children walk from square to square around the circle. Then stop the music and have the children look underneath the squares they are standing on. Whichever child has the different shape gets to decide on the next activity or be first for the next activity.

VARIATION: Have the children sit in a circle and pass around one shape to music. When the music stops, the child holding the shape gets to be dismissed for hand washing, snack, or the next activity.

Heart Tree

Stand a tree branch in a pot of soil. Ask your children to name ways they can show love and kindness to others; for example, by helping to put away toys or by sharing with friends. Then have each child dictate a sentence to you telling you how he or she will show kindness to someone else. Print each child's sentence on a separate paper heart. Hang the hearts on the tree branch with string or yarn to create a Heart Tree.

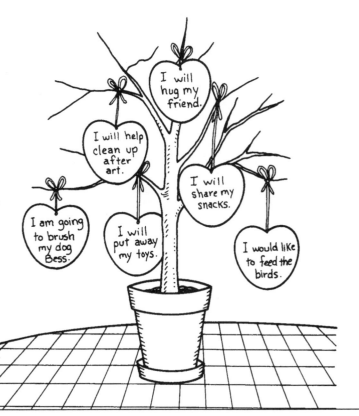

Trip Tip

When planning a field trip for your children, write the destination and departure on a paper school bus shape. Attach this shape to the sign-up sheet to attract parents' attention.

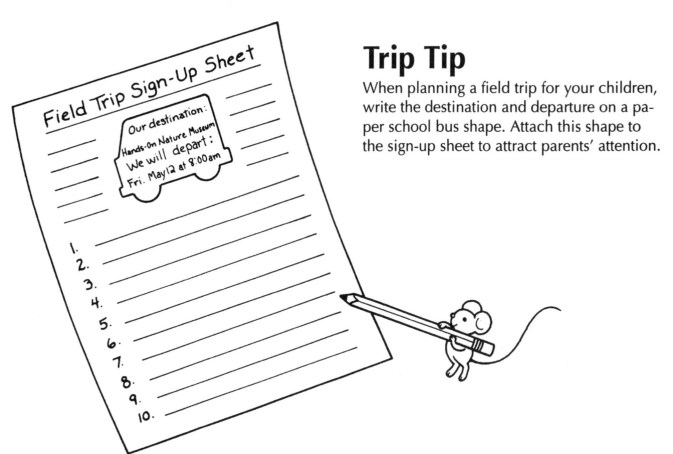

ART

Party Crowns

Cardboard borders are the perfect width for making crowns, and the cardboard is sturdier than construction paper. To make crowns for parties and other special occasions, cut a piece of border big enough to fit around each child's head. Have the children decorate their border with stickers or other materials as desired. Staple the ends of the border together to form a crown. Before the children wear their crowns, cover any exposed staples with tape.

VARIATION: To turn crowns into wigs, attach strands of yarn along the bottom edge of the crown. You may wish to make several wigs, each in a different style. For example, to make a ponytail, attach long strands of yarn to the back of the crown. To make a curly wig, attach loops of yarn.

Cloud Mobiles

Provide each of your children with a section of blue border. Set out cotton balls and glue. Have your children stretch out the cotton balls and glue them on the border sections to make cloud designs. If you wish, have the children glue tinsel underneath the clouds to represent rain. When the borders are dry, staple the ends of each border together with the design facing out. Punch holes in the top of each border with a hole punch and string yarn through the holes for hanging.

Lacy Art

Give each of your children a 12-inch piece of plain red border. Have the children punch holes in the border pieces with a hole punch to make designs. Then have the children attach their border pieces to sheets of white paper, revealing the lacy designs made by the hole punch. Help the children trim the paper to fit the border. These make beautiful room decorations for Valentine's Day.

Cooperative Borders

Provide each of your children with a section of border in the same solid color. Have the children glue paper scraps, buttons, cotton balls, or other materials to their border sections. When the border sections are dry, arrange them end-to-end around a bulletin board, window, or other area of your room. Your children will take pride in their group effort.

Framed Masterpieces

Set out sheets of construction paper and border pieces precut to fit the edges of the paper. Let each of your children select a sheet of paper and four border pieces. Have the children glue the border pieces around the edges of the paper to make frames. Encourage them to draw or paste pictures inside their frames.

VARIATION: Provide photographs or photocopied poems for the children to place inside their frames.

Wavy Rubbings

From a roll of corrugated border with a scalloped edge, cut a piece of border slightly wider than a sheet of paper. Tape the border to a table with loops of masking tape. Have one of your children place a piece of paper over the border. Show the child how to rub the side of a peeled crayon over the paper to make a Wavy Rubbing. Let the child move the paper slightly and rub again with a contrasting color. Continue until each child has made a rubbing.

EXTENSION: Let the children add paper fish shapes to their drawings to make ocean scenes.

Ocean Waves Bulletin Board

Have your children fingerpaint with blue and green paint on large sheets of paper. Attach these paintings to a bulletin board. Then fasten strips of scalloped blue border at random on the board to look like waves. Let your children add paper fish shapes and other sea creatures to the bulletin board, tucking some behind the border strips to transform the bulletin board into an underwater world.

Look Through My Window

Use borders to make a window frame (11 by 17 inches) on a wall in the housekeeping center or another area of your room. Throughout the year, invite one of your children to draw a picture on an 11-by-17-inch sheet of paper of what he or she imagines is outside the window. Mount the picture inside the frame. Have the child tell the rest of the group about the drawing, if he or she wishes.

LANGUAGE

Accordion Book

Fold a section of solid-colored border into an accordion shape. Attach a sticker or small picture to each folded section. Let your children unfold the book and make up a story about the pictures inside. Display the Accordion Book where all can see it.

Sequence Stories

Cut a section of border into three pieces. On each piece, attach a different magazine photograph or other picture. Invite your children to arrange the border pieces and tell stories incorporating the pictures. Have your children rearrange the pieces whenever they wish to tell a new story.

Alphabet Board

Cut strips of solid-colored border into 3-inch pieces. Using a permanent marker, write a letter of the alphabet on each piece. Attach a piece of magnetic strip to each. Let your children use these letters on a magnetboard. Encourage them to look for the letters in their names.

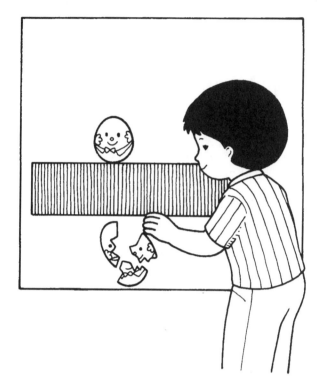

Humpty Dumpty Sat on a Wall

To make Humpty Dumpty's wall, cut a strip of corrugated border to fit on a flannelboard. Then set out identical paper egg shapes. Decorate each shape to look like Humpty Dumpty. Cover these shapes with clear self-stick paper for durability. Cut one of the Humpty Dumpty shapes into a few pieces. Attach small squares of sandpaper to the back of the border and each flannelboard piece. As you recite the Humpty Dumpty rhyme, use the flannelboard pieces to illustrate the story. Let your children take turns making Humpty Dumpty fall from the wall. Later, have the flannelboard pieces available for children to make up their own stories about Humpty Dumpty.

EXTENSION: Set out pieces of border, paper egg shapes, crayons, glue, and sheets of paper. Have the children use these materials to make Humpty Dumpty pictures.

LEARNING GAMES

Teaching Border

Use a permanent marker to divide a solid piece of border into six or more sections. On opposite sides of each dividing line, draw matching shapes, patterns, or letters. Cut out the sections. Then let your children piece the border together by finding things that match.

Twin Crowns

Make a crown from a solid-colored border for each of your children. Divide the crowns into pairs and decorate them with matching stickers. Distribute the crowns among your children. Have the children hold the crowns in their hands and try to find the child with a matching crown. Let the children with Twin Crowns be partners for the next activity.

Texture Crowns

Give your children precut pieces of solid-colored border to make crowns. Cut textured materials, such as sandpaper, fabric scraps, or cotton balls, into small pieces. Let the children glue combinations of these materials on their border pieces. Help them staple the ends of their borders together to make crowns. Encourage the children to touch their crowns and describe the various contrasting textures.

Color Crowns

When learning a new color, have your children celebrate that color on a special day. Have the children make crowns for their color celebration. For example, on Red Day, let the children make crowns out of red borders and decorate them with scraps of red construction paper and red ribbons.

VARIATION: Have your children decorate crowns with newly learned shapes or numbers.

Curvy Challenge

Cut two identical pieces of scalloped border. Place the two scalloped edges together, offsetting the strips so that they fit snugly. Trim the top and bottom ends away. Then attach matching stickers to the border sections along the scalloped edges. Now cut the sections into puzzle pieces and let your children put them back together by matching the stickers.

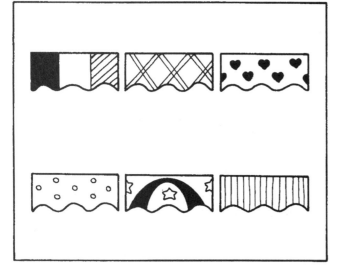

Lotto

Set out pieces of six different scalloped borders. Cut one section from each border. Glue these pieces onto posterboard in two rows of three. This will be the gameboard. Cut six matching pieces of border to use as game cards. Attach a large envelope to the back of the gameboard to store the game cards. Make as many different game sets as you wish. Give the game to one of your children and have the child try to place each game card on the corresponding section of the gameboard.

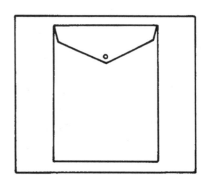

Concentration

Gather five or six pieces of assorted scalloped borders. From each piece of border, cut a pair of identical matching cards. Turn the cards over and spread them out on the floor or on a tabletop. Let your children take turns selecting two cards. If they match, have the child lay them face up. If they do not match, have the child put the cards back exactly as they were and try again. Continue until all the cards have been matched.

Alpha-Match Puzzles

Collect several border strips in solid colors. Cut each strip into two sections. Then cut each section into three interlocking pieces. Use a permanent marker to print an uppercase letter on the left-hand piece and a matching lowercase letter on the right-hand piece. On the middle piece, attach a picture of something whose name begins with the printed letter. Set out several puzzles at a time and let your children sort the pieces and put the puzzles together.

Matching Puzzles

Collect an assortment of printed borders. First cut the borders into 8-inch lengths and then cut each length into two interlocking pieces. Mix up the pieces and let your children put the puzzles back together. This is a great way to reuse leftover bulletin board materials.

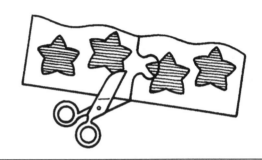

Flower Pot Match

Attach borders around the rims of five plastic flower pots. Make one large dot on the first border, two large dots on the second border, etc. Write the numerals 1 to 5 on enough flower shapes so that each child will get one. Glue each of these flowers on a craft stick. Distribute the flowers among your children. Invite the children to sit on the floor and then come up one at a time to plant their flower in the appropriate pot.

Shape Counting Book

From a piece of shape border, cut a single shape. Write the numeral 1 on this shape. Then cut a strip with two shapes. Number these shapes 1 and 2. Continue with strips of three, four, and five shapes. Stack the shapes in order with the shortest on top, and staple them together to make a booklet. Let your children take turns counting the shapes on each page.

VARIATION: Make a book from two different shape borders to show an alternating pattern when the book is closed.

Number Squares

Cut a section of solid-colored border into ten pieces. Separate the pieces into two sets of five. With a permanent marker, draw dots on the first set of border pieces. Draw one dot on the first piece, two dots on the second piece, and so on. On the second set of pieces, use the same procedure to draw Xs or another contrasting mark. Attach a piece of magnetic strip to the back of each piece. Let your children arrange the pieces on a magnetboard, matching the pieces that have corresponding numbers of dots and marks or putting them in ascending or descending order.

Measuring Sticks

Cut border pieces to match the length of various things in the room, such as an aquarium, a cubby, or a window. Let your children select a border piece and search the room to see if they can find some thing that is the same length as that border section.

So Big

Measure each child's height. Let each of your children select a colored or patterned border from an assortment of borders. (Each child will need at least two identical pieces of border.) Cut each child's border to his or her height. Glue these borders on sheets of butcher paper to make a bar graph comparing the heights of your children.

Jorgé   Cecily   Maria   Brian   Kelly

Number Line

Tape border strips together to make a long number line. With a permanent marker, mark off ten sections and number them. With your children, count the numbers on the number line. Then set out a stuffed animal. Have your children take turns moving the animal a specific number of spaces along the number line. For example, you might ask a child to help the animal walk from 1 to 3. Help the children understand that as the animal moves along the number line, the numbers get bigger or smaller.

Number Strips

Cut a shape border into three strips of five shapes each. Cut the first strip into two shorter strips of one shape and four shapes. Cut the second strip into two strips of two shapes and three shapes. Leave the third strip as is. Mix up all the strips and give them to one of your children to play with. Have the child try to line up the strips from longest to shortest. Then point to the longest strip. Let the child try to put together two strips to equal that length.

TIPS

Attendance Tags

Make a nametag for each of your children by writing his or her name on a piece of border with a permanent marker. You may wish to use borders in an assortment of shapes and colors to make it easier for children to identify their tags. Punch two holes in the top of each nametag with a hole punch. Loop yarn through the holes. Have your children hang their nametags on a pegboard to show that they are present each day.

Center Tags

If you have learning centers in your program, use nametags to help your children tell at a glance whether there is space available in a center. From borders, make nametags for your children. Punch a hole in each nametag and tie a loop of yarn through the hole. Near each center, display a pegboard with hooks representing the number of spaces in the center. When the children work in a center, have them hang their nametags on the hooks. As they move from one center to another, they will know that only those centers with empty hooks have available space.

Welcome Tag

When a new child enters your program, make a nametag for him or her using a border. Write "Welcome (child's name)" or another greeting on the tag and tape it to the child's clothing. Remind the other children to be particularly helpful to the new child as he or she learns the layout of the school and the names of new friends.

HINT: Borders preprinted with the word "Welcome" make this activity even easier.

Calendar Countdown

At the beginning of each month, count the number of school days the month contains. Then display a shape border containing one shape for each day your children will be in school. At the end of each school day, cut one shape off the border. This helps children understand the concept of passing time. The cut-off shapes can be kept and used for other activities.

Waiting Line

Attach a strip of border to the floor of your classroom about 3 feet from the door. This line will help remind your children where to stand as they wait in line to leave the room. You may also wish to put several borders end to end to make a long line for children to stand along as they wait.

VARIATION: Make waiting lines in other areas where children must wait, such as near the sink or bathroom.

Designer Borders

Use a craft knife to cut seasonal shapes out of solid-colored borders. These borders give a stenciled effect to a bulletin board covered with contrasting paper. The shapes that were cut out may be used for bulletin boards or other displays.

VARIATION: Use a craft punch to cut designs in borders. Save the cutout pieces for collages and other art projects.

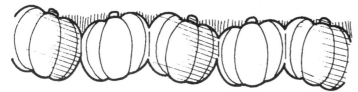

Three-Dimensional Borders

Before putting a border on a bulletin board, fold it accordion style. Stretch the border out just far enough that the folds give the border a three-dimensional effect. This works especially well with shape borders.

I Did It!

When one of your children masters a new skill, such as cutting with scissors, tying shoelaces, or learning his or her address, drape a star-patterned border around the child to resemble a beauty contestant's sash. Make another strip of star-patterned border into a crown. Let the child wear the crown and sash for the remainder of the day to signify his or her accomplishment.

Book Binding

When your children make books, have them glue strips of border along the stapled edge of the front and back covers. In addition to protecting fingers from sharp staples, the colorful borders make the book more durable.

Border Cards

To make a delightful greeting card or gift enclosure, cut a shape border apart after every two shapes. (The shapes must be identical.) Fold the border in half and write a message on the inside.

VARIATION: To make a three-dimensional card, cut a 3-by-6-inch strip of construction paper. Fold the construction paper in half to make a square card. Then cut a single section (a 3-inch square) from a pop-out border. Fold out the perforated areas, then glue the square of border to the construction paper card.

Washboard Blocks

Glue a strip of corrugated border, rippled side up, to a wooden block or other smooth piece of wood. Let your children scrape along the cardboard ridges with a metal spoon to make a washboard sound.

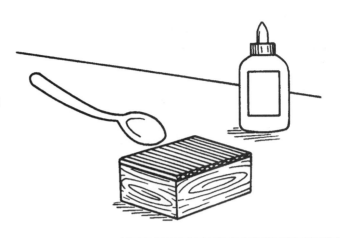

Crepe Paper Skirt

Cut a strip of border long enough to go around a child's waist. Attach strips of crepe paper to the border to make a skirt. Punch a hole in both ends of the border with a hole punch and tie a piece of cloth ribbon to each end. Let your children wear this skirt for dramatic play activities.

Sand Combs

Cut scalloped borders into 6- to 12-inch strips to make inexpensive toys for the sandbox or sand table. Let your children drag the scalloped edge of the border through the sand to make interesting ripple patterns.

TEACHING THEMES

BUSY BEES

For Two's and Three's
Day-by-day, hands-on projects and activities are just right for busy little ones.

Busy Bees—FALL
For fall fun and learning, these attention-getting activities include songs, rhymes, snacks, movements, art, and science projects. 136 pp.
WPH 2405

Busy Bees—WINTER
Enchant toddlers through winter with a wealth of seasonal ideas, from movement to art. 136 pp.
WPH 2406

Busy Bees—SPRING
More than 60 age-appropriate activities enhance learning for busy minds and bodies. 136 pp.
WPH 2407

Busy Bees—SUMMER
Encourage toddlers to build, develop, and explore with their senses and turn summer fun into learning. 136 pp.
WPH 2408

CELEBRATIONS

Expand on your children's love for celebrations with these ideas for special learning fun.

Small World Celebrations
Multicultural Units • 160 pp.
WPH 0701

Special Day Celebrations
Nontraditional Units • 128 pp.
WPH 0702

Yankee Doodle Birthday Celebrations
Antibias Units • 128 pp.
WPH 0703

Great Big Holiday Celebrations
Traditional Units • 228 pp.
WPH 0704

PLAY & LEARN

This creative, hands-on series explores the versatile play and learn opportunities of a familiar object. Perfect for working with young children ages 3 to 8. Each 64 pp.

Play & Learn with Photos
WPH 2303

Play & Learn with Magnets
WPH 2301

Play & Learn with Rubber Stamps
WPH 2302

THEME-A-SAURUS

Capture special teaching moments with instant theme ideas that cover around-the-curriculum activities.

Theme-A-Saurus
50 teaching themes—from Apples to Zebras—plus 600 fun and educational activity ideas. 280 pp.
WPH 1001

Theme-A-Saurus II
Sixty more teaching units—from Ants to Zippers—for hands-on learning experiences. 280 pp.
WPH 1002

Toddler Theme-A-Saurus
Sixty teaching themes combine safe, appropriate materials with creative activity ideas. 280 pp.
WPH 1003

Alphabet Theme-A-Saurus
From A to Z—26 giant letter recognition units filled with hands-on activities introduce young children to the *ABC's*. 280 pp.
WPH 1004

Nursery Rhyme Theme-A-Saurus
Capture the interest children have for nursery rhymes and extend it into learning. 160 pp.
WPH 1005

Storytime Theme-A-Saurus
Flannelboard patterns accompany 12 storytime favorites, plus hands-on activities and songs. 160 pp.
WPH 1006

EXPLORING SERIES

Environments
Selected environments become very real places in this book series that encourages exploration. Hands-on activities emphasize all the curriculum areas. Each book begins with the "known" and lets the curriculum expand as far as children's interests can stretch.

Exploring Sand and the Desert
WPH 1801

Exploring Water and the Ocean
WPH 1802

Exploring Wood and the Forest
WPH 1803

TEACHER RESOURCES

1001 SERIES

These super reference books are filled with just the right solution, prop, or poem to get your projects going. Creative, inexpensive ideas await you!

1001 Teaching Props
The ultimate how-to prop book to plan projects and equip discovery centers. Comprehensive materials index lets you create projects with recyclable materials. 248 pp.
WPH 1501

1001 Teaching Tips
Shortcuts to success for busy teachers on limited budgets. Curriculum, room, and special times tips—even a subject index. 208 pp.
WPH 1502

1001 Rhymes & Fingerplays
A complete language resource for parents and teachers! Rhymes for all occasions, plus poems about self-esteem, families, special needs, and more. 312 pp.
WPH 1503

1•2•3 SERIES

These books present simple, hands-on activities that reflect Totline's commitment to providing open-ended, age-appropriate, cooperative, and no-lose experiences for working with preschool children.

1•2•3 Art *Open-ended Art*
160 pages of art activities emphasize the creative process. All 238 activities use inexpensive, readily available materials. 160 pp.
WPH 0401

1•2•3 Colors
Hundreds of activities for Color Days, including art, learning games, language, science, movement, music, and snacks. 160 pp.
WPH 0403

1•2•3 Books
More than 20 simple concept books to make, including sequences, textures, and weather. 80 pp.
WPH 0406

1•2•3 Murals *Cooperative Art*
More than 50 simple murals to make from children's open-ended art. 80 pp.
WPH 0405

1•2•3 Reading & Writing
250 meaningful and non-threatening activities to develop pre-reading and pre-writing skills. 160 pp.
WPH 0407

BEAR HUGS SERIES

This unique series uses a positive approach for dealing with potential problem times. Great ideas for handling specific group situations. Each 24 pp.

Remembering the Rules
These simple rule reminders are fun and nonthreatening.
WPH 2501

Staying in Line
Make staying in line fun, quiet, and safe.
WPH 2502

Circle Time
Get children interested and involved in circle time.
WPH 2503

Transition Times
Help children smoothly shift focus from one activity to another.
WPH 2504

Time Out
Encourage reflective and therapeutic time outs that get results!
WPH 2505

Saying Goodbye
Ease separation anxiety with simple activities and gentle distractions.
WPH 2506

Nap Time
Guide reluctant children into quiet, restful moods.
WPH 2509

Meals and Snacks
Quiet young ones so they can eat without dampening their spirits.
WPH 2507

Cleanup
Encourage cooperation and speedy work with fun cleanup times.
WPH 2508

1•2•3 Rhymes, Stories & Songs *Open-ended Language*
Open-ended rhymes, stories, and songs for young children. 80 pp.
WPH 0408

NEW! 1•2•3 Shapes
Hundreds of activities for exploring the concept of shapes—circles, squares, triangles, rectangles, ovals, diamonds, hearts, and stars. 160 pp.
WPH 0411

1•2•3 Math
Hands-on activities, such as counting, sequencing, and sorting, help develop pre-math skills. 160 pp.
WPH 0409

1•2•3 Science
Develop science skills—observing, estimating, predicting—using ordinary household objects. 160 pp.
WPH 0410

1•2•3 Games *No-Lose Games*
Foster creativity and decision-making with 70 no-lose games for a variety of young ages. 80 pp.
WPH 0402

1•2•3 Puppets
More than 50 simple puppets to make to delight children. 80 pp.
WPH 0404

Instant Hands-on Ideas!

Totline® Newsletter and **Super Snack News** are perfect for working with young children because they are put together by the publisher of Totline® Books, a leader in early childhood resources for parents and teachers. Totline books and newsletters are guaranteed to be appropriate, enriching, and fun. Help your children feel good about themselves and their ability to learn by using the hands-on approach to active learning found in these two newsletters!

Warren Publishing House
P.O. Box 2250, Dept. Z, Everett, WA 98203

Totline® Newsletter

This newsletter offers creative hands-on activities that are designed to be challenging for children ages 2 to 6, yet easy for teachers and parents to do. Minimal preparation time is needed to make maximum use of common, inexpensive materials. Each bimonthly issue includes • seasonal fun • learning games • open-ended art • music and movement • language activities • science fun • reproducible teaching aids • reproducible parent-flyer pages and • Good Earth (environmental awareness) activities. *Totline Newsletter* is perfect for use with an antibias curriculum or to emphasize antibias values in a home environment.

Super Snack News

This newsletter is designed to be reproduced!

With each subscription you are permitted to make up to 200 copies per issue! They make great handouts to parents. Inside this monthly, four-page newsletter are healthy recipes and nutrition tips, plus related songs and activities for young children. Also provided are category guidelines for the CACFP reimbursement program. Sharing *Super Snack News* is a wonderful way to help promote quality childcare.

To receive your FREE copy of either Totline Newsletter or Super Snack News, call 1-800-773-7240.